CAREGIVING REALTY

An Adult Child's Experience with Long-Term Care Insurance

Carolyn Olson, CLTC

Carolyn Olson, CLTC
Visit my website at www.TheCarolynOlson.com

Printed in the United States of America

First Printing: May 2022
Independently published

ISBN- 9798816604598

In remembrance of mom, a journey I would gladly do again.

—CAROLYN

CONTENTS

In remembrance of mom, a journey I would gladly do again.

—CAROLYN

AUTHOR'S NOTE

This book is very personal to me. It is my story of a wonderful and emotional season of my life. My intention with this book is to help other families understand the costs of long-term care, how insurance works and the blessing of caring for your family.

As a licensed insurance agent specializing in long-term care insurance, I find myself routinely talking about my experience as a caretaker for my mom. From filing the claim for my mother, to moving her into the assisted living facility, then moving her into my home, I have lived the long-term care experience and know first-hand the value of long-term care insurance.

Buying insurance is a logical, rational, and financial decision. Woven together, though, is the emotional aspect of long-term care. No one wants to admit or think about needing care. Yet without a firm plan in place, you are leaving your family with the stress and difficulty of making those decisions for you.

I hope my story inspires you to provide a long-term care plan for your family, one that includes a plan for the financial aspect of needing care.

THE CALL

I t all started with "The Call." I clearly remember where I was when my life changed with the call. After traveling all day from our home in Washington state, my husband and I had just landed in Florida for a business conference. I powered up my cell phone, and there was a text from my brother asking me to call him. I knew.

I had my normal video chat with my parents the day before, just like I did every Saturday morning since moving to Washington from my hometown in Southern California. During the video chat, I thought my mother's speech was weird a few times. I would peer closely at the screen to see if her face looked different. This happened several times during the one-hour call. I never said a word because I assumed that my dad would say something if anything were wrong. I mean, he was sitting right next to her. If she were talking weird, he would notice and say something. Right??

So, when I saw my brother's text asking me to call him when I had a chance, I knew. My parents had planned that day to see my brother's family, so I knew.

Funny enough, the first thing my brother asked was if I had noticed anything about mom's speech during our video call the day before. He had just spent hours with her, noticed something off, and didn't say anything either. It wasn't until he was back home that his wife asked him about it.

No one wanted to admit mom's speech was different. Since I was in Florida, we agreed that he would simply show up in the morning and take her to the ER to get checked out. No sense in everyone losing sleep. As the only daughter, I was nominated to call mom and tell her the plan.

Talk about denial! Mom and dad seemed very surprised that we had noticed anything unusual about mom's speech. They both maintained there was nothing out of the ordinary. Mom felt fine, a little tired, but okay. Dad said he hadn't noticed anything different. But they were very willing to cooperate.

My brother took mom to the ER that next day, and I made plans to fly to California from Florida the following day. I knew there had been some kind of mild stroke or TIA (trans-ischemic attack). Nothing good would cause my mother's speech to be off. I had to be there in California for her.

This call changed my life and began a story of long-term care. It impacted my family's life – all my family's life.

BACKSTORY – MY PARENTS

These are my parents. This photo was taken in May 2017, precisely two weeks before my father almost died of septic shock. Despite their age and physical limitations, my parents had traveled alone from California to Wisconsin for a family wedding. At this point, my father had already survived numerous health crises. Two weeks after this family wedding, my father had his gallbladder removed, and two days later, his fever spiked, and his blood pressure fell. We all thought we'd lose him.

To better understand this story, I need to go back several years.

Before I met and married Scott Olson, I had never heard about long-term care insurance. At age 35 with three children, it was definitely not on my radar. My parents were in their late 60s and very independent and private financially. At that time, I didn't know the importance of asking them if they had a plan for long-term care costs. That changed once I met Scott.

When my father learned that Scott was an insurance agent specializing in long-term care insurance, he only commented that he planned to "self-insure." When my dad retired from the Air Force, he investigated the federal long-term care plan. His opinion was that it was expensive, and they would never need it.

My dad didn't realize that "self-insuring" actually meant "*self-funding*" for long-term care costs. During the one conversation we had about it, he said that he planned to start selling his rental houses if he or my mother needed care. Scott was never in the practice of selling to friends and family, so the subject was left there.

My father's motivation in life was to care for his family, especially my mother. His main goal was to provide their retirement with passive income, hence the rental houses. He had been building a moderate nest egg of four rental houses to complement his military pension, social security, and VA disability income. He steadfastly guarded that passive income. I'm sure he weighed the risks of needing care with the risk of restricting their income and thought he was safe.

As the years passed, my dad got tired of managing the rental houses and considered selling them. That idea lasted all of a day when he realized how much he'd be paying in capital gains to the federal and state governments. There went his plan for self-funding long-term care costs. It would have cost him about $100,000 in taxes per rental house if he sold his investment properties. Therefore, his new plan was to let me sell the homes after they died, and there was a new cost basis.

In this realization, my father decided to investigate long-term care insurance. His health prevented him from qualifying for a policy, but my mother was healthy enough to purchase a policy. Scott compared quotes for her, and the federal long-term care plan was the best and least expensive choice. At age 68, my mother purchased a modest 3-year policy with a future purchase option as inflation protection.

As the years passed, my father executed the purchase option as specified in the policy: they purchased 10% more coverage every two years. This increased the premium, but they planned to use mom's monthly social security to pay the premium. They were able to set the payments up, then forget about it until they got the next purchase option letter.

As my parents aged into their late 70s, and I became a licensed insurance agent myself specializing in long-term care insurance, I knew that my dad's plan for self-funding his care would ruin his careful retirement planning. But there was nothing else to be done except possible Medicaid planning, but that would entail selling a rental house to fund an annuity. He just would not consider giving the government over $100,000 in taxes. After every continuing education class of mine, I would again hope and pray that my father never needed long-term care because it would drastically change everything about the financial freedom they were enjoying in retirement.

Following my mother's knee replacement in her mid-70s, her scoliosis became worse, altering her gait and affecting her balance. Over the next few years, she began to move slower and slower. Then, we all noticed that her short-term memory was starting to fade. When we siblings would talk about it, we would ask each other, "What's up with mom?" There was no answer.

At age 79, she suffered a minor stroke, and I received "The Call." The MRI and CT scans showed cerebral amyloid angiopathy (CAA) and that my mother had 12-15 prior brain bleeds. CAA brings with it a terrible prognosis of dementia and physical challenges. It was sobering, to say the least.

This brings me back to that family wedding in Wisconsin, about three months after mom's minor stroke. My father asked Scott and me, "What should we do about mom?" Our immediate response was, "Make a long-term care insurance claim!" Most people want to wait to start the claims process "until they really need it." Well, she needed it. The plan was to provide my mother with home health care - stand-by assistance for bathing and dressing.

Stand-by assistance means that someone needed to be within arm's reach to keep my mother safe. My father had already started to remain in the bedroom while my mother showered and dressed. But that only meant he would know right away if she fell. The idea was to keep mom safe before she fell.

My father agreed that starting the long-term care insurance claim made the most sense. His gall bladder removal surgery was scheduled a week after the wedding, so he planned to start the claim after the surgery. But before my father could make the call to begin the process, he developed double pneumonia and sepsis. In the span of a few hours, my father went from being entirely independent to not being able to get himself out of bed. Needless to say, he almost died.

Within three months, I received "The Call" for a second time. This time I was kayaking with one of my sons. It was a gorgeous June day in the Pacific Northwest, I was kayaking with my adult son, and my world changed again. While on the kayak, I made my plane reservation on my phone to leave the next day. I knew that both my parents now needed care, and I was the one to arrange it.

THE CLAIMS PROCESS – WHAT TO DO

While he was still in the hospital, I dug out mom's long-term care insurance policy and met with Amada Senior Care, a home health care company that also assists with the filing of long-term care insurance claims. I had met the founder of Amada Senior Care at a business conference and knew that this company provided this service free of charge. Although I was an expert in helping people shop and compare long-term care insurance, I was *not* an expert in filing long-term care insurance claims.

Amada Senior Care, and other home health care agencies, had a staff whose only job was to help people file long-term care insurance claims. Amada Senior Care sent their claims expert to my parents' home, my mother signed a few forms, and Amada handled the rest. Within 10 days or so, a nurse called to arrange the certification in-home interview with my mother, and within five weeks, I had a phone call that her claim had been approved.

Since they purchased their policy in 2006, I hadn't given it much thought. I was pleasantly surprised to learn that my mother had used the future purchase option to buy more coverage, and her modest policy had grown to be $344 per day. This amounts to $10,320 per month in benefits for three years, totaling over $376,000 of benefits. I knew that this policy would be more than adequate to cover the care my mother needed. This is the gift of long-term care insurance – the ability to arrange care without too much thought to cost.

Not only did my mother need assistance with bathing, dressing, and daily walks, but my father needed someone available 24/7 due to his weakened condition. Because my mother's long-term care insurance policy had a 90-service day elimination period, **Amada Senior Care** billed the care separately for each of my parents. That way, I would be able to

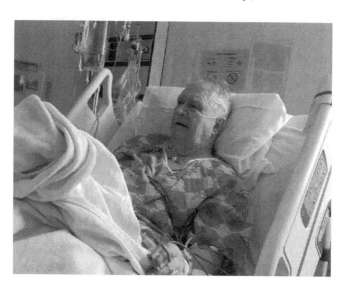

send the invoice for only mom's portion to the insurance company for reimbursement.

Miraculously, my father recovered from the infections, although he was weaker than he used to be. Fortunately, he only needed home health care for about four weeks, and he had the cash available in savings to pay his bill. I think my father willed himself to recover quickly because he didn't want to continue spending $36 per hour for his care. As it was, he spent about $10,000 on his home care. Yes, he could've gone to a rehab, skilled nursing facility directly from the hospital, which would have saved him money. But, a few years earlier, he had a bad experience with a rehab nursing facility, and we all vowed he would never go to one again.

After getting my parents settled with the caregivers, I needed to return to Washington. It was a tough decision because I instantly became their rock, decision maker, confidante, and counselor. Before I came home, we notarized two essential documents: Durable Power of Attorney and Durable Power of Attorney for Health Care. These documents named me as their power of attorney (POA) for financial issues and health-related decisions, should either one not be in a position to decide for themselves. Both documents are needed since one is for medical decisions and the other is for finances. Both documents named me as the primary POA acting with sole discretion.

THE ALF DECISION

O nce I was back home, I knew they needed to move to an assisted living facility (ALF). Why did I know that? Within three months, my mother had a minor stroke, and we learned of the CAA diagnosis, and my father's health turned quickly. From previous discussions with my mother, I knew that my mom wanted to live near me if anything happened to my father. It just made sense that it was time for them to live where there was help nearby.

So, Scott and I toured the two facilities near our home. Again, despite being in the business of long-term care insurance, neither of us had any idea there was a difference in facilities.

The first facility we toured immediately told us that there was a 6-9 month waiting list. This was very concerning because my parents needed assistance now and paying for home health care for my father would be expensive. When we toured the facilities, we didn't know how long my father would need care. We couldn't wait 6-9 months. However, once that facility learned that my mother had a long-term care insurance policy, we were told she was first on the waiting list for the next available apartment. The long-term care insurance policy meant paying cash to the facility, not relying on Medicaid, so we were moved to the top of the list.

We toured the second facility in our community, and we mentioned my mother's long-term care insurance policy right away. There was never mention of a waitlist. We were shown the units that were available and given a price list. A ground floor 2-bedroom, 2-bathroom unit was coming available that included a washer and dryer inside the unit. Although apartment living would be drastically different and smaller than my parents were used to, it was the best available in the area. Scott and I provided the check deposit to hold the unit for my parents, even though we hadn't yet discussed it with them.

In talking with my father during the next week, I brought up the possibility of moving into an ALF. He wasn't too thrilled about leaving his home, a 4-bedroom house that he had lovingly fixed up to be his perfect retirement oasis. I know he understood the benefit of the ALF and said that he'd discuss it with mom. To say that I hated this discussion is an understatement. My love for my parents compelled me to act on my instinct to help them get settled into a safe environment. It had already been demonstrated more than once that they couldn't help each other should one of them fall or need help.

Because we all saw firsthand how quickly things could change, my parents made the hard decision to move to the ALF here in Washington. My father had made it his life's ambition to care for my mother. He wanted to ensure that she was in a good place should something suddenly happen to him again.

My siblings and I were able to counsel my parents and assist them with this life-altering decision without considering the cost of care because of my mother's long-term care insurance policy. We had peace of mind knowing that my mother would have the care she needed as she got older, lost more memory, or her mobility continued to decline. We had peace of mind knowing that if something happened to my father and he needed care, it wouldn't affect my mother's care.

With the help of us kids, my parents packed up their retirement house, giving away lots of stuff and downsizing to fit everything into the 2-bedroom/2-bathroom apartment at the ALF near my home. They even went shopping for a new bed to be delivered to their new home. I negotiated with the management to have the apartment custom painted with the colors from their house, so it looked and felt more like home. It was lovely.

HOW LONG-TERM CARE INSURANCE WORKS

Once the decision was made to move to the ALF, I needed to finalize the arrangements with the facility. This was the first time I used the Durable POA document, for which the facility needed a copy. Then, I was given paperwork asking me every imaginable question about my parent's health, well-being, diet, education, preferences, habits, etc. Fortunately, I was close to my parents and knew most of the answers.

It was from these answers that the care plan for my mother emerged. Again, this was the first time I acted as their surrogate, making decisions for them. I determined what care mom needed. I chose what days and times for her shower and the time of her dressing each day. I decided whether my mother needed anyone to walk with her to the dining room or not or needed help with her medication. It was daunting, to say the least.

When it was time to sign the contract for their unit, I was given a separate form and told to take my time reading it. This particular form asked for my personal information: full name, address, social security number, and driver's license number. I was shocked to learn that there is always someone financially guaranteeing the contract. As the POA, that someone was me.

I was able to sign the contract personally, guaranteeing it with confidence, knowing that the long-term care insurance policy would pay most of the cost. If there had not been a long-term care insurance policy, that experience of guaranteeing over $5,000 per month would have been very stressful for Scott and me.

Because my mother needed assistance with 2 of the 6 activities of daily living (ADLs), 100% of the cost of their 2-bedroom apartment was covered by my mother's long-term care insurance policy. Basic rent for the apartment was $4,200 per month. The cost of care (bathing and dressing for my mother) was $685 per month. My father's portion was $785 per month to cover his three meals per day. All of this was separated clearly on the monthly invoice from the facility.

When they moved into the ALF, we had already paid about 60 service days of home healthcare for my mother. My parents only paid out-of-pocket for the ALF for one month, then the long-term care insurance policy began reimbursing them for the expense. Each month the facility mailed the invoice directly to me. I would scan and email the invoice to the insurance claims department, and within 10-14 days the claim was processed, and a direct deposit was made into my parents' bank account. It was very easy.

My only other responsibility to the insurance company, other than to send them the invoice every month, was to alert them if mom's health changed. If she ever needed to be in the hospital overnight, it was my responsibility to inform the claims coordinator at the insurance company of any days that she was not living in the ALF. Again, it was very easy to do, but it was a responsibility I was assuming.

ALF REALITY

Because my parents had moved a significant distance, they needed new doctors. Before the big move, I went to all of their doctor's offices and requested hard copies of their medical records to hand carry to their new doctors. From primary care doctors to their dentists and optometrist, I gathered their medical records and canceled all future appointments. Like most aging seniors, my parents had numerous appointments pre-scheduled that needed canceling. At times, it was overwhelming the sheer number of details that needed addressing before this move to an ALF in a different community.

I found a cardiology specialist for my father, had his records transferred and scheduled an appointment shortly after they arrived at the ALF. My dad was given a completely clean bill of health. Everyone was amazed at his miraculous recovery from double pneumonia and sepsis only nine weeks prior. My father set about settling their belongings and hanging pictures – creating a home for them.

The day after meeting his new cardiologist, my father passed away peacefully in his sleep, only six days after moving into the ALF with my mother.

I was driving to meet a friend for coffee when my mother called and said, "I think your father is dead." She gave the phone to the paramedic, who asked me what to do – should they resuscitate him, or did he have a DNR? As my father's newly appointed POA for Health Care, it was up to me to decide. After having experienced the previous few months with him, I absolutely knew the answer. So, as I drove to the facility, I told the paramedics to stop resuscitating my father. That is how I learned of my father's passing.

The paramedics and staff were still in the apartment waiting for the coroner when my mother asked if she would have to move. Because of her long-term care insurance policy, I confidently told her that she never needed to move. I am so grateful to my father for buying my mother's long-term care insurance policy. Thanks, Dad.

After my father's passing, my mother settled into her new life at the assisted living facility. It was a difficult journey for her, especially without my father. She didn't like people coming into her apartment to help her shower and dress every day, but she understood the need for safety. Establishing a new routine for lunches and dinners in a dining room seemed like grade school again. Some incredibly lovely ladies reached out to her after my father's passing. They assured her that there was a place for her at their table each meal.

It took a few months, but the routine was set: Be Fit exercise class each morning, followed by a walk around the building (or walking the halls if the weather was bad), then lunch at 11am, then Bible study at 1pm on Tuesdays and Thursdays.

I also settled into a routine, bringing her to my home on Sundays and Mondays. On Thursdays, I would visit her at the ALF and stay for lunch. Saturdays, we would take her out to eat at a restaurant. This was to be our routine, our very comfortable routine.

Each month, the long-term care insurance did what it was designed to do – pay for my mom's long-term care costs. The invoice each month was the same: rent and cost of care. What I didn't realize during that summer we moved my parents into the ALF was the cost of inflation each year. Each January, the facility raised the cost of the rent and care by 3-6%. When I asked about it, I was told that although the state's inflation index was less than 3%, and inflation was very low at that time, the cost of health care services was rapidly increasing. There seemed to be a constant shortage of health care workers, especially Licensed Vocational Nurses (LVN) and Certified Nursing Assistants (CNA).

Regardless of the rate increases each year, I could bank nearly all of my mother's income each month. She could freely spend her money on herself or her grandchildren without a budget. As her POA, I was responsible for managing all her money, including my parents' investment properties. In addition, I also managed my mother's health, taking her to doctor appointments and filling her prescription medi-sets. I saved my mother about $800 per month by doing it myself. However, this only worked because my mother was good at taking her medicines each morning and evening. The ALF offered the medication management service, which was an excellent service for people who forgot to take their medicine.

I wouldn't describe my mother's care at the ALF as perfect. There probably isn't such a thing as perfect long-term care. Just when my mother would get attached to a particular caregiver, that person would be transferred or leave the job. Truly loving and caring licensed caregivers are not common.

Most of the people providing stand-by or hands-on assistance for my mother were very nice and probably did their best.

My mother was very independent by nature. One should never forget that no matter how aged or infirm their loved ones become, they used to be someone in their youth. Caregivers that spoke to ALF residents as children grated on me, and my mother tolerated them. Again, I believe they were doing their best, given the situation. But every resident I met at the ALF had fascinating stories to tell from their families and careers before their need for assisted care.

Throughout this first year of her living at the ALF as a recent widow, she was still very much MY MOTHER. I found it difficult at times to be the caretaker she needed me to be. It was a role I needed to grow into. Fortunately, my mom was a gracious woman who made it easier for me.

For example, one day, I had brought her over to my home, and while enjoying the gorgeous summer day sitting on the deck, I noticed what looked like mud on her lower leg around her ankle. I racked my brain to figure out where my mother could've walked that morning to get mud on her ankle. My mind was in denial of the truth. Although I knew mom struggled with urinary continence and saw evidence of toileting issues at her apartment, I didn't want to acknowledge what I was seeing. And I certainly didn't want to embarrass my mom by asking her about her toileting abilities. I felt awful, but I never said anything to her. To my shame, I let her finish the day with dried poop on her ankle.

The next day, we walked across the street from the ALF together for a routine doctor appointment. I got up the guts to talk to her about it, stating very plainly that we can't live like that – if I saw something like poop on her leg, I needed to say something, and she needed to let me. Again, her poise and grace saved my aching heart. It was me that needed to expand into the role and become her caretaker and she lovingly told me to do and say what needed to be done. She gave me permission to be that person for her.

Then, COVID-19 happened.

LONG-TERM CARE IN A POST-COVID WORLD

When our state shut down, I followed the guidelines and didn't visit my mother or bring her to my home. For 30 days, I only saw my mom on a video call or from her back porch as I dropped off groceries or supplies. (Her apartment was on the ground floor with a separate exterior entrance.) However, I must share the difficulties I experienced with the staff at the ALF during this time. As my mother's Durable Power of Attorney for Health Care and as a member of her caregiving team, I handled all of her medications, including a weekly B12 injection.

The facility refused to allow me to administer the injection, choosing to interpret our governor's guidelines as disallowing me as a medical advocate and caregiver. It was all fine, as they took over the weekly injections with no cost. But I knew, and they knew, that they would not touch her medications, assemble her medi-sets or ensure that mom was actually taking her medications. Thus began the challenge all facilities had during the difficult times of the COVID shutdown.

Every five weeks, I would refill her medi-sets, entering her apartment from the separate entrance, thus obeying the "no visitor" rule. And the facility never questioned me again about the medications.

Once the stay-home order lifted, I resumed my weekly visits with my mother to check her medications and overall health. I'm glad I did because she developed a bladder infection during this time which the facility caregivers missed. I don't blame them at all. They were short-staffed with many residents stuck indoors getting weaker and weaker during the COVID rules imposed by the ALF corporate office.

Because of the separate private entrance into my mother's apartment, I was able to help her get diagnosed and treated on the same day. Unfortunately, she reacted to the medication and fell that evening, resulting in a 3-day hospital stay. Nothing was broken, but it did take her several weeks to recover.

During this time, I began to bring her to my home three days per week. We would inform the facility that she was leaving and everything was okay or as acceptable as things could be for her. The dining room was shut down. There were no activities allowed in the facility. No visitors were allowed in the facility. My mother was unable to walk the halls. Don't get me wrong, I clearly understood why the facility needed to make these decisions, but it was extremely hard for my mother and all residents. She missed seeing her friends even though nothing stopped her from walking around the building to her friend's porch and chatting with her there. To my knowledge, she only did it once.

Side note: I later learned that not all assisted-living facilities had rules like this. Scott and I toured another facility in a nearby community, and that facility never shut down its dining room or activities during COVID. We even considered moving her to that facility to give her the lifestyle that she needed to remain active.

As the summer of 2020 progressed, it was clear that COVID wasn't going anywhere and that this indeed was the new normal for my mother and me. Bringing her to my home three days per week, and driving her back, certainly changed things for us. But it was a pleasure to do it for her instead of simply letting her be alone all that time.

In mid-August 2020, the ALF was just beginning to open up activities for residents again. My mother had returned to the exercise class as the one activity that gave her daily routine. One day while leaving the class, a staff member gave her a paper that described a scoring of sorts weighing a resident's COVID risk to the community. She was told that if she left the community to come to my home, she would be quarantined for 14 days each time. Or, she could stop doing the daily activities in the community and still leave the facility without being quarantined.

It was cruel. Everything about COVID was/is brutal, but our seniors in long-term care facilities bore the greatest burden. My mother was in tears.

 Our choice was easy, and my husband Scott made it even easier. Upon hearing about this turn of events, Scott grabbed my mother's rollator (walker) and started wheeling it around our house, through the bedroom doorway turning into the bathroom. He was testing it to see how easy it would be for her to maneuver around our house if she lived with us. There was no discussion except when we could do it and how we would convert the shower/tub into a step-in shower. And this is where my mother's long-term care insurance policy came into play again.

ALF TO HOME CARE

N o one said that caregiving was easy. Yet, after talking with hundreds of clients, most everyone assumes and expects to receive care in their home. And I agree that remaining at home is ideal; it's perfect for the person needing care and for their family to be able to see them every day. However, the family bears the added weight of responsibility.

As an insurance agent specializing in long-term care insurance, I talk with people every week who tell me that they never want their children to care for them. In reality, loved ones will do what is necessary to assist. Rarely does someone qualify for long-term care insurance (needing assistance with 2 of the 6 ADLs) and need care only a few days per week. The reality is that someone qualifying for a long-term care claim will need assistance every day, possibly only a few hours per day, but care is needed every day. And finding reliable, caring home health care providers seven days per week is challenging, especially in suburban or rural areas.

Once the decision was made to move my mother into our home, I called the long-term care insurance company and informed them of our decision and the estimated date of her moving. The company's care coordinator called me and thoroughly explained the home care benefits of her policy to me, which were slightly different than the benefits offered for the ALF. Side note: make sure you purchase a long-term care insurance policy with 100% facility and 100% home care benefits

Mom's policy offered an "alternate plan of care" and family caregiver benefits. Because of COVID and the shortage of caregivers nationwide, the insurance company allowed family members to provide care. Normally, her policy would have allowed a family member to be paid for only one year. Due to COVID, however, the insurance company allowed an unlimited period for family members to be paid to provide care. It is important to note that someone besides the family member needed to sign the claim forms to reimburse a family member for care provided.

We set about renovating the bathroom, moving an adult child from one bedroom to another, and getting her room ready. It was fun for my mom to choose the paint color and new bedspread to match. This plan gave her something to look forward to, yet there was stress involved. Since there are no sidewalks in our rural area, could she walk alone in our neighborhood? Should she walk alone? Did she need an emergency pendant to wear around her neck? What about call buttons in her bedroom if she needed something at night? What kind of food did I need to buy for her lunches, and who would make it?

Regarding the bathroom and bedroom remodel, the "alternate plan of care" in the long-term care insurance policy allowed modifications to the home. Although my mother did not own this house, her long-term care insurance policy paid over $8,000 towards the renovations in our home for removing the bathtub and tiling a shower. This provision also covered the cost of installing grab bars where needed in our home.

Submitting the claim for the home modification was easy – I simply sent the invoices and receipts for the bathroom remodel, and the grab bars purchased, and the insurance company reimbursed my mother. Obviously, this "alternate plan of care" in her long-term care insurance policy was needed and made the transition easier for us all.

After buying call buttons from Amazon and setting up the emergency call pendant, Mom moved in with us on September 15, 2020. I had hired a home health care agency to provide 4 hours of care for my mother each morning, Monday through Saturday, to help her bathe and dress, help her exercise, go for a walk, and prepare her lunch. Since we worked from home, I was available if she needed anything in the afternoons or evenings. I provided care on Sundays.

It was the perfect plan, and we all expected this to last for at least five years. But excellent plans rarely go according to plan. The home healthcare agency had difficulty finding caregivers in my rural area and only staffed three days of the first week Mom lived with us. By the second week, I was searching for a private caregiver on Care.com and found someone to supplement the days the agency couldn't provide.

Life was good. We all settled into a routine of sorts. I would stop working around 4pm each day to make dinner, and we would watch a show together while we ate dinner. If I worked late, my mother would stand in my office doorway and look at me, asking if it was time to move from her room to the living room for dinner. We all hugged her each morning, and Scott instigated "paying the toll" as my mother walked from the living room to her bedroom after dinner each night. He would block her way with his arm until she kissed him on the cheek. It was lovely watching them develop their own relationship living together.

We only had two weeks of this new normal before things changed again for us.

THE REALITY OF HOME CARE

On September 29, 2020, my mother experienced an episode of syncope. It was awful. Scary. Syncope means "loss of consciousness", but it really looks like the person died – everything stops. She regained consciousness, but her blood pressure was very low. Since we didn't know what had happened, she was transported to the hospital via ambulance. This experience taught me that I needed the Physician Orders for Life-Sustaining Treatment (POLST) form for my mother taped to the refrigerator. I'll come back to this later.

Once mom was home again, she was weaker than usual, so the doctor ordered physical therapy, occupational therapy, and speech therapy. Now, I was juggling my mother's schedule of multiple weekly visits from these therapists. Because of this health event, my mother needed more care during the day, so I increased the home care agency's hours from 4 to 6 hours per day.

With all the stress about my mother's health, I didn't have to worry about the money. Her long-term care insurance policy allowed me to decide to increase her care without considering cost and without lengthy explanations to my brothers about why I was spending more money. However, explaining the need for more care to my mother proved the most challenging conversation.

Although mom had given me permission to be her caretaker in all that it meant, she didn't really want anyone to help her. My mother had earned her BS in Nursing in 1959 and joined the US Air Force as an officer wanting to see the world. In fact, she was photographed for Life Magazine to promote other ladies to join the armed forces. There were very few women officers at this time, and my mother relished the role.

What kind of woman did it take to leave the simple life in Billings, Montana and join the Air Force? She was strong and independent, and no shrinking violet. Yet everyone who met my mom at the ALF told me how sweet she was. Sweet? Until that time, I had never heard my mom described as sweet. And I didn't know her as sweet. Kind and gracious, yes, but not sweet.

So, having a conversation with her to explain why I needed to increase her care up to 6 hours per day was very difficult. As a licensed insurance agent, I explained the activities of daily living to my clients all the time. But I never thought about what the ADL "toileting" meant. Like I've said, I was in denial about it. While she lived at the ALF, I could ignore it unless I was visiting when something happened. Mom was stubborn enough that she never, and I mean never, pulled the cord to ask for assistance when she needed it. She tolerated help every morning and evening to get dressed and undressed, but if she needed to change her briefs or pants during the day, she did it herself. And she would make attempts to clean the floor or toilet herself, but she really couldn't do it.

Once she lived in my home, though, there was no denial. And she still wouldn't ask for help. There were call buttons by every chair she used, by her bed, and next to the toilet. With me, she rarely used it. Therefore, I couldn't trust her in the bathroom. If she had an incontinence event, she wouldn't call me. So, I increased her care so I could work uninterrupted – without worrying and without bending one ear to the bathroom, constantly wondering if she needed help. The caregiver was much better at getting her to cooperate than I. Obviously. Who wants their daughter to help them in the bathroom with personal hygiene?

The caregiver was an essential part of my mother's care, not just in the bathroom but helping me to manage the weekly therapy appointments. Getting and keeping the right caregiver was vitally important, and I did find a local CNA who re-arranged her schedule to be available five days per week. To make things easier on my mother, I was her caregiver Saturdays and Sundays.

This became our new routine for a few months until the next health crisis changed things again.

Without my mother's long-term care insurance policy, the next saga of my mother's living with us would have been a nightmare. Her policy allowed me to increase her care even more without considering the cost. I knew the policy limit for home care, and I increased the private caregiver to the greatest number of hours the policy would allow. And I chose to provide care myself all the other hours, including weekends.

On December 28, 2020 my mother had a GI bleed during the night. Did she press her call button to alert Scott and me? No. She didn't want to wake us up. Instead, she went back to sleep and continued to bleed until morning, when an odd odor filled the house, waking us all up. Yes, blood has a smell.

This is where the need for a POLST form comes into play. After the last transport to the hospital in September, we completed the POLST form, with my mother choosing "no heroics". It was to be full DO NOT RESUSCITATE (DNR) under any circumstances. This form was with her at the ER following the GI bleed.

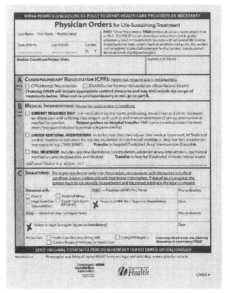

The bottom line is that the ER staff always defaults to saving someone's life, not making them comfortable. They disregarded my mother's DNR on the POLST form and brought her blood pressure back when it fell. It just wasn't her time yet. But this is important to note: discuss the POLST form, know what it says, and remember that an ER will always want to save someone's life, not do nothing.

In the days that followed the GI bleed, the caregiver was diligent in monitoring my mother's health. Her vitals were taken 1-2 times per day, and she was constantly being assessed for bladder infections. Apparently, once seniors reach a certain age, the symptoms of bladder infections are often not felt. Instead, bladder infections in seniors present as cognitive impairment or confusion. With mom's mild dementia due to the CAA diagnosis, it was often a challenge to know if it was simply "not a good day" for mom's cognition or a bladder infection.

On many days, the caregiver would show me her vitals, and we would wonder why her temperature was elevated or her blood pressure was lower than usual. The worst days were trying to decide if mom needed medical assistance: did she actually have a bladder infection, should we lower her blood pressure medication, and did she need loperamide for diarrhea or a stool softener? Each day brought new decisions, all of which rested on me. The stress on me personally was something I hadn't anticipated.

During this time, Scott's sister-in-law passed away due to cancer. I knew we needed to be there for Scott's brother. It was difficult enough to find caregiving for ordinary days, let alone arrange care for my being absent from the home for five days. I negotiated with the caregiver to be there every day, all day, and for a family friend to visit a few times each day. One of my adult children was to stay at the house with mom, with the other kids nearby if anything happened. It wasn't a perfect plan, but it allowed me to remain with Scott as we traveled across the country for the funeral.

When we left for the airport and we drove down the street, I made it three minutes before I started crying. The sheer weight of being solely responsible for mom's care and well-being was heavier than I realized. Leaving her for five days was worse than leaving my young children for five days! Scott fully expected the tears as he seemed to understand more than I the strain I had been under. As that weight lifted with each passing mile away from home, I could emotionally relax in ways that I hadn't for months.

HOSPICE – A DIFFERENT PLAN OF CARE

From January to April my mother never got her strength back from that GI bleed. Her doctors wanted to do more

tests to evaluate how best to help her. All the while, my mother was withdrawing, almost depressed at times. She spent her days much the same every day yet found little joy in things that used to interest her. She knew she needed to exercise and walk but had no interest. Instead, she listened to books on Audible or watched the same repeated shows on Netflix.

By the end of April, I heard somewhere that hospice might be an option simply to have a different care plan. It was not giving up, nor even an expectation of impending death, but merely a change from saving or improving someone's life to keeping them comfortable. My mother was all for it, and it took the stress off me.

The morning after the doctor's video visit establishing the order for hospice, my mother was beaming. She was thrilled to know that she wouldn't ever have to go to the hospital again. The hospice nurse came out for the evaluation and reviewed everything with my mother. As her Healthcare POA, I was always the one explaining things and talking with

healthcare providers. But not this hospice nurse. Their job was to ensure the patient knew exactly what was happening and evaluate the need. My mother was approved for hospice care on April 25, 2021. The long-term care insurance policy continued to pay for the cost of the caregiver, while Medicare paid for the hospice nurses and medications.

I'll never know exactly what my mom was thinking during this time. I tried to engage her in conversations about her life, asking about her Air Force days, what it was like being discharged from the military simply because she was pregnant with my brother, why she never returned to the nursing profession, etc. I even asked her to tell me the story of how she met my father. All my life, when that story was told, it was my

father who would tell it. She didn't say much, but her version shed light on her quiet yet strong personality.

My mother declined every single day once she was approved for hospice, and she passed away on May 20, 2021. Although it was fast, it also felt long and drawn out. It was awful to watch, yet such a blessing to be with her those final weeks.

The caregiver would arrive at 8am and leave at 4:30pm Monday through Friday. Until this time, I would always be the caregiver on the weekends, but now our wonderful CNA offered to be there on Saturdays to assist me. With her rapid decline to being bedridden, I was unprepared to handle the tasks.

Again, mom's long-term care insurance paid the cost of care every day, and I didn't have to worry about money at all

during this emotional time. Her caregiver played such an essential role during this time, both as a support to my mother and to me and my family; I truly cannot fully express the depth of emotion and connection that happens during such a time. Hospice was amazing. The home health caregiver was amazing. And I am left with good memories of my mother's final days with us.

FINAL THOUGHTS

I am passionate about long-term care insurance. I've lived it. I've seen it play out from the start of a claim to the end of the claim, and I've experienced the relief it brought to my family and me. Not worrying about the financial aspect of aging and dying has no dollar value. When I deliver a long-term care policy to my clients, I am often asked about the claims process. It always seems to come as a surprise when I remind them that they will likely not be the one actually filing the claim – it will be their spouse, child, or other loved one. I hope that this little booklet will be left with long-term care insurance policies to be read by those loved ones making the decisions.

So again, thank you, Dad, for buying long-term care insurance for mom.

APPENDIX

Questions Caretakers Need Answered

What is needed to keep my loved one safe?
What kind of care is needed?
Where should the care be provided?
Who is best to provide care?
What does the long-term care insurance policy pay for home care?
Is there a monthly maximum amount for home care, or is it capped each day?

Home Care Considerations

- Are home modifications needed to keep your loved one safe?
- Grab bars – where needed and how many?
- Bathroom: ADA height toilet, hand-held or automatic bidet to help with toilet hygiene, flushable wipes, storage nearby for continence items, step-in or walk in shower, hand-held shower nozzle, any shower assist hygiene items, gloves and adult personal wipes to assist toilet hygiene
- Call buttons
- Emergency call pendant
- POLST form
- Bed pads
- Transfer wheelchair
- Lap desk or TV trays for meals or snacks